WEAPON SYSTEMS CYBERSECURITY (GAO-19-128) October 2018

DOD Just Beginning to Grapple with Scale of Vulnerabilities

This report presents the argument that Department of Defense (DOD) weapons systems under development are riddled with vulnerabilities that make them an easy target for adversaries trying to control them or disrupt their functions. GAO was asked to review the state of DOD weapon systems cybersecurity. This report addresses:

(1) factors that contribute to the current state of DOD weapon systems' cybersecurity,

(2) vulnerabilities in weapons that are under development, and

(3) steps DOD is taking to develop more cyber resilient weapon systems.

Of course, a test on systems still under development is not the same as a fully-developed system that is ready for deployment. One can assume that DoD is doing everything possible to ensure that weapons cannot be hacked. This report is a good assessment of the size of the problem and should not be considered an indictment of the unfinished products.

Why buy a book you can download for free? We print this book so you don't have to.

First you gotta find a good clean (legible) copy and make sure it's the latest version (not always easy). Some documents found on the web are missing some pages or the image quality is so poor, they are difficult to read. We look over each document carefully and replace poor quality images by going back to the original source document. We proof each document to make sure it's all there – including all changes. If you find a good copy, you could print it using a network printer you share with 100 other people (typically its either out of paper or toner). If it's just a 10-page document, no problem, but if it's 250-pages, you will need to punch 3 holes in all those pages and put it in a 3-ring binder. Takes at least an hour.

It's much more cost-effective to just order the latest version from www.Amazon.com

This material is published by 4th Watch Publishing Co. We publish tightly-bound, full-size books at 8 ½ by 11 inches, with large text and glossy covers. 4th Watch Publishing Co. is a Service Disabled Veteran Owned Small Business (SDVOSB). Please visit www.usgovpub.com.

Other books available on www.Amazon.com:

GAO Green Book (GAO-14-704G) - Standards for Internal Control in the Federal Government

GAO Yellow Book (GAO-17-313SP) - Government Auditing Standards

GAO Financial Audit Manual (GAO-18-601G)

GAO Technology Readiness Assessment Guide (GAO-16-410G)

GAO Cost Estimating and Assessment Guide (GAO-09-3SP)

DoD 7000.14 - Financial Management Regulation

Defense Acquisition Guidebook (Chapters 1 - 10)

Federal Acquisition Regulation - Complete

Defense Federal Acquisition Regulation – Complete

OMB No. A-123 - Management's Responsibility for Enterprise Risk Management and Internal Control

OMB A-130 & Federal Information Security Modernization Act (FISMA)

Federal Information System Controls Audit Manual (FISCAM)

Report to the Committee on Armed Services, U.S. Senate

October 2018

WEAPON SYSTEMS CYBERSECURITY

DOD Just Beginning to Grapple with Scale of Vulnerabilities

GAO-19-128

Highlights of GAO-19-128, a report to the Committee on Armed Services, U.S. Senate

WEAPON SYSTEMS CYBERSECURITY

DOD Just Beginning to Grapple with Scale of Vulnerabilities

Why GAO Did This Study

DOD plans to spend about $1.66 trillion to develop its current portfolio of major weapon systems. Potential adversaries have developed advanced cyber-espionage and cyber-attack capabilities that target DOD systems. Cybersecurity—the process of protecting information and information systems—can reduce the likelihood that attackers are able to access our systems and limit the damage if they do.

GAO was asked to review the state of DOD weapon systems cybersecurity. This report addresses (1) factors that contribute to the current state of DOD weapon systems' cybersecurity, (2) vulnerabilities in weapons that are under development, and (3) steps DOD is taking to develop more cyber resilient weapon systems.

To do this work, GAO analyzed weapon systems cybersecurity test reports, policies, and guidance. GAO interviewed officials from key defense organizations with weapon systems cybersecurity responsibilities as well as program officials from a non-generalizable sample of nine major defense acquisition program offices.

What GAO Recommends

GAO is not making any recommendations at this time. GAO will continue to evaluate this issue.

View GAO-19-128. For more information, contact Cristina Chaplain, 202-512-4841, chaplainc@gao.gov

What GAO Found

The Department of Defense (DOD) faces mounting challenges in protecting its weapon systems from increasingly sophisticated cyber threats. This state is due to the computerized nature of weapon systems; DOD's late start in prioritizing weapon systems cybersecurity; and DOD's nascent understanding of how to develop more secure weapon systems. DOD weapon systems are more software dependent and more networked than ever before (see figure).

Embedded Software and Information Technology Systems Are Pervasive in Weapon Systems (Represented via Fictitious Weapon System for Classification Reasons)

Targeting systems

Industrial control systems

Identify friend or foe systems

Database

Microelectronics throughout

Flight software system

Controller Area Network bus

Communications systems

Source: GAO analysis of Department of Defense information. | GAO-19-128

Automation and connectivity are fundamental enablers of DOD's modern military capabilities. However, they make weapon systems more vulnerable to cyber attacks. Although GAO and others have warned of cyber risks for decades, until recently, DOD did not prioritize weapon systems cybersecurity. Finally, DOD is still determining how best to address weapon systems cybersecurity.

In operational testing, DOD routinely found mission-critical cyber vulnerabilities in systems that were under development, yet program officials GAO met with believed their systems were secure and discounted some test results as unrealistic. Using relatively simple tools and techniques, testers were able to take control of systems and largely operate undetected, due in part to basic issues such as poor password management and unencrypted communications. In addition, vulnerabilities that DOD is aware of likely represent a fraction of total vulnerabilities due to testing limitations. For example, not all programs have been tested and tests do not reflect the full range of threats.

DOD has recently taken several steps to improve weapon systems cybersecurity, including issuing and revising policies and guidance to better incorporate cybersecurity considerations. DOD, as directed by Congress, has also begun initiatives to better understand and address cyber vulnerabilities. However, DOD faces barriers that could limit the effectiveness of these steps, such as cybersecurity workforce challenges and difficulties sharing information and lessons about vulnerabilities. To address these challenges and improve the state of weapon systems cybersecurity, it is essential that DOD sustain its momentum in developing and implementing key initiatives. GAO plans to continue evaluating key aspects of DOD's weapon systems cybersecurity efforts.

_____ **United States Government Accountability Office**

Contents

Abbreviations

DOD	Department of Defense
DOT&E	Director of Operational Test and Evaluation
DSB	Defense Science Board
IT	Information Technology
NSA	National Security Agency
NIST	National Institute of Standards and Technology
RMF	Risk Management Framework

GAO

U.S. GOVERNMENT ACCOUNTABILITY OFFICE

441 G St. N.W.
Washington, DC 20548

October 9, 2018

The Honorable James M. Inhofe
Chairman
The Honorable Jack Reed
Ranking Member
Committee on Armed Services
United States Senate

The Department of Defense (DOD) plans to spend about $1.66 trillion to develop its current portfolio of weapon systems.[1] These weapons are essential to maintaining our nation's military superiority and for deterrence. It is important that they work when needed, yet cyber attacks have the potential to prevent them from doing so. Cyber attacks can target any weapon subsystem that is dependent on software, potentially leading to an inability to complete military missions or even loss of life. Examples of functions enabled by software—and potentially susceptible to compromise—include powering a system on and off, targeting a missile, maintaining a pilot's oxygen levels, and flying aircraft. An attacker could potentially manipulate data in these systems, prevent components or systems from operating, or cause them to function in undesirable ways.

Some advanced threat actors are aware of this and have well-funded units that focus on positioning themselves to potentially undermine U.S. capabilities. For example, according to the National Security Agency (NSA), advanced threats are targeting national security systems. According to the Department of Homeland Security's U.S. Computer Emergency Readiness Team and industry reports, advanced threats may conduct complex, long-term cyber attack operations. These reports show that threats may employ cyber reconnaissance, such as probing systems, and cyber espionage, such as cyber theft, to develop detailed knowledge of the target system to design and deploy more damaging attacks.

---

[1]We use "weapon systems" and "acquisition programs" to refer to major defense acquisition programs. These include a broad range of systems, such as aircraft, ships, combat vehicles, radios, and satellites. They are programs that are estimated to require a total expenditure for research, development, test, and evaluation of more than $480 million, or for procurement of more than $2.79 billion, in fiscal year 2014 constant dollars, for all increments or are designated as such by DOD for oversight purposes. For more information, see GAO, *Weapon Systems Annual Assessment: Knowledge Gaps Pose Risks to Sustaining Recent Positive Trends,* GAO-18-360SP (Washington, D.C.: Apr. 25, 2018).

Furthermore, in 2017, the Director of National Intelligence testified that some adversaries remain undeterred from conducting reconnaissance, espionage, influence, and even attacks in cyberspace.[2]

Cybersecurity is the process of protecting information and information systems by preventing, detecting, and responding to attacks. It aims to reduce the likelihood that attackers can access DOD systems and limit the damage if they do.[3] Since 1997, we have designated federal information security—another term for cybersecurity—as a government-wide high-risk area.[4] We have also reported and made hundreds of recommendations on a wide range of topics related to cybersecurity, such as information security programs across the federal government, privacy of personally identifiable information, critical infrastructure, and federal facility cybersecurity.[5] We have found that the federal government needs to, among other things, improve its abilities to detect, respond to, and mitigate cyber incidents and expand its cyber workforce planning and training efforts.

You asked us to conduct a series of reviews on DOD's efforts to improve the cybersecurity of the weapon systems it develops. This report addresses (1) factors that contribute to the current state of DOD weapon systems cybersecurity, (2) vulnerabilities in weapons that are under development, and (3) steps DOD is taking to develop more cyber resilient weapon systems. We focused primarily on weapon systems that are under development.

---

[2]Coats, *Worldwide Threat Assessment of the US Intelligence Community*, testimony delivered to the Senate Select Committee on Intelligence on May 11, 2017.

[3]Definition adapted from National Institute of Standards and Technology, *Framework for Improving Critical Infrastructure Cybersecurity*, Version 1.1 (Apr. 16, 2018).

[4]GAO, *High-Risk Series: Information Management and Technology*, GAO/HR-97-9 (Washington, D.C.: February 1997); and *High-Risk Series: Urgent Actions Are Needed to Address Cybersecurity Challenges Facing the Nation*, GAO-18-622 (Washington, D.C: Sept. 6, 2018).

[5]See for example: GAO, *Federal Information Security: Agencies Need to Correct Weaknesses and Fully Implement Security Programs*, GAO-15-714 (Washington, D.C.: Sept. 29, 2015); *Information Security: IRS Needs to Further Improve Controls over Financial and Taxpayer Data*, GAO-16-398 (Washington, D.C.: Mar. 28, 2016); *Critical Infrastructure Protection: Additional Actions Are Essential for Assessing Cybersecurity Framework Adoption*, GAO-18-211 (Washington, D.C.: Feb. 15, 2018); *Federal Facility Cybersecurity: DHS and GSA Should Address Cyber Risk to Building and Access Control Systems*, GAO-15-6 (Washington, D.C.: Dec. 12, 2014).

To identify factors that contribute to the current state of DOD weapon systems cybersecurity, we reviewed reports issued from 1991 to the present on software, information technology (IT), networking, and weapon systems from the National Research Council, the Defense Science Board (DSB), GAO, and other organizations as well as key DOD policies and guidance. To identify vulnerabilities in weapon systems under development, we reviewed cybersecurity assessment reports from selected weapon systems that were tested between 2012 and 2017.[6] To determine the steps DOD is taking to develop more cyber resilient weapon systems, we analyzed DOD information assurance/cybersecurity, acquisition, requirements, and testing policies and guidance that have been updated since 2014, when DOD began more concerted efforts to address weapon systems cybersecurity.

To inform each objective, we interviewed Office of the Secretary of Defense officials, including Office of the Director, Operational Test and Evaluation; Office of the Deputy Assistant Secretary of Defense for Developmental Test and Evaluation; Office of the Chief Information Officer including the Defense Information Systems Agency; Office of the Chairman of the Joint Chiefs of Staff; Office of the Under Secretary of Defense (Acquisition and Sustainment) and Office of the Under Secretary of Defense (Research and Engineering).[7] We interviewed officials from all military test organizations, NSA, and DOD program offices. To select the program offices, we used a purposeful sample of 9 major defense acquisition programs representing each service, multiple domains, and programs that are extensively connected to other weapons systems.[8] We

---

[6]Because of the time it takes to develop weapon systems, operational test results from this time period should generally reflect outcomes of DOD's cybersecurity policies and practices prior to recent changes.

[7]In response to Section 901 of the National Defense Authorization Act for Fiscal Year 2017 (Pub. L. No. 114-328), DOD is restructuring the office of the Under Secretary of Defense for Acquisition, Technology and Logistics. Effective February 1, 2018, that office was reorganized into two separate offices: the Under Secretary of Defense (Research and Engineering) now advises the Secretary on key investments to retain technical superiority based on the analytical rigor and understanding of risk associated with these technologies; and the Under Secretary of Defense (Acquisition and Sustainment) advises the Secretary on all matters regarding acquisition and sustainment and is involved in the oversight of individual programs as required.

[8]A purposeful sample is also known as non-generalizable or judgmental. These samples can be used to provide contextual sophistication and illustrative examples, among other purposes.

also interviewed other organizations with cybersecurity expertise. See appendix I for additional information on our scope and methodology.

To present information in an unclassified format, we do not disclose details regarding weapon system vulnerabilities, which program offices we interviewed, or which cybersecurity assessments we reviewed. The examples we cite from cybersecurity assessments are unique to each weapon system and are not applicable to all weapon systems. Furthermore, cybersecurity assessment findings are as of a specific date, so vulnerabilities identified during system development may no longer exist when the system is fielded. In addition, we illustrated some concepts using fictitious depictions. In some cases, we were deliberately vague and excluded some details from examples to avoid identifying specific weapon systems. We also presented examples of publicly known attacks in sidebars to illustrate how poor cybersecurity can enable cyber attacks. DOD conducted a security review of the report and cleared it for public release. We will provide a classified briefing of our findings to Congress.

This is our first report specific to cybersecurity in the context of weapon systems acquisitions. For that reason, we did not look in depth at related issues in the context of weapon systems, such as the security of contractor facilities, so-called "Internet of Things" devices, microelectronics, contracting, and industrial control systems.[9] In addition, we are not making recommendations in this report, but plan to continue evaluating key aspects of DOD's weapon systems cybersecurity efforts in the future.

We conducted this performance audit from July 2017 to October 2018 in accordance with generally accepted government auditing standards. Those standards require that we plan and perform the audit to obtain sufficient, appropriate evidence to provide a reasonable basis for our findings and conclusions based on our audit objectives. We believe that the evidence obtained provides a reasonable basis for our findings and conclusions based on our audit objectives.

---

[9]GAO has issued reports related to some of these topics, but not specific to weapon systems cybersecurity. See for example GAO, *Internet of Things: Enhanced Assessments and Guidance Are Needed to Address Security Risks in DOD*, GAO-17-668 (Washington, D.C.: July 27, 2017); *Trusted Defense Microelectronics: Future Access and Capabilities are Uncertain*, GAO-16-185T (Washington, D.C.; Oct. 28, 2015); and *Defense Infrastructure: Improvements in DOD Reporting and Cybersecurity Implementation Needed to Enhance Utility Resilience Planning*, GAO-15-749 (Washington, D.C.: July 23, 2015).

Background

Weapon Systems Are Unique In Many Ways, but Face Common Cyber Vulnerabilities

Cybersecurity issues can vary widely across different types of systems, so weapon systems cybersecurity challenges may be very different than those of some IT systems. Despite variation across systems, cybersecurity can be described using common terminology, such as the key terms below used by the National Research Council.[10]

- **A cyber vulnerability** is a weakness in a system that could be exploited to gain access or otherwise affect the system's confidentiality, integrity, and availability.[11]

- **A cybersecurity threat** is anything that can exploit a vulnerability to harm a system, either intentionally or by accident.

- **Cybersecurity risk** is a function of the threat (intent and capabilities), vulnerabilities (inherent or introduced), and consequences (fixable or fatal).

Although some weapon systems are purely IT systems, most—such as aircraft, missiles, and ships—are what the National Institute of Standards and Technology (NIST) and sometimes DOD refer to as "cyber-physical systems." NIST defines these systems as "co-engineered interacting networks of physical and computational components."[12] These cyber systems can affect the physical world so the consequences of a cyber attack may be greater than those of attacks on other types of systems. For example, an attack on a weapon system could have physical consequences that may even result in loss of life.

---

[10]Unclassified terms and definitions from classified report. National Research Council of the National Academies, *A Review of U.S. Navy Cyber Defense Capabilities* (Washington, D.C.: National Academies Press; 2014).

[11]Confidentiality means limiting information and system access to authorized users and purposes. Integrity means ensuring information is not modified or deleted by unauthorized users. Availability means ensuring information and services are available to authorized users.

[12]NIST definition, see www.nist.gov/el/cyber-physical-systems. DOD also sometimes uses the term "platform information technology," which the NSA defines as IT, both hardware and software, that is physically part of, dedicated to, or essential in real time to the mission performance of special purpose systems.

Nevertheless, weapon systems share many of the same cyber vulnerabilities as other types of automated information systems. Weapon systems are large, complex, systems of systems that have a wide variety of shapes and sizes, with varying functionality.[13] Despite obvious differences in form, function, and complexity, weapon systems and other types of systems are similar in some important, if not obvious, ways. For example, DOD reports state that many weapon systems rely on commercial and open source software and are subject to any cyber vulnerabilities that come with them. Weapon systems also rely on firewalls and other common security controls to prevent cyberattacks. Weapon system security controls can also be exploited or bypassed if the system is not properly configured. Finally, weapon systems are operated by people—a significant source of cybersecurity vulnerability for any system.[14]

Anatomy of a Cyber Attack

One common way to discuss cybersecurity is through the activities necessary to defend (or attack) a system. System developers and operators take steps to protect the system from cyber attacks, while attackers attempt to defeat those protections as depicted in figure 1. The cyber attack sequence is also referred to as a cyber kill chain or cyber attack lifecycle. There are multiple models for understanding cyber attacks, each with their own terminology and sequence of steps. The attack sequence below is simpler, but generally consistent with existing cybersecurity models.[15] We identified the defend sequence below based on the steps included in cybersecurity test reports that we reviewed.[16]

---

[13]See GAO, *Weapon Systems Annual Assessment: Knowledge Gaps Pose Risks to Sustaining Recent Positive Trends*, GAO-18-360SP (Washington, D.C.: Apr. 25, 2018).

[14]GAO, *Information Security: Agencies Need to Improve Controls over Selected High-Impact Systems*, GAO-16-501 (Washington, D.C.: May 18, 2016).

[15]For other examples of attack sequences, see the Office of the Director of National Intelligence's Cyber Threat Framework, Lockheed Martin's Cyber Kill Chain, and Mandiant Consulting's Cyber Attack Lifecycle.

[16]NIST's *Framework for Improving Critical Infrastructure* identifies five cybersecurity functions: "identify," "protect," "detect," "respond," and "recover." The "identify" function is defined as developing the organizational understanding necessary to manage cybersecurity risk. We have not included the "identify" function in our defend sequence because it is an organization-level function whereas the other functions focus on preventing or responding to a cybersecurity event, as depicted in Figure 1.

Figure 1: Key Activities in Cyber Attacks and Cyber Defense

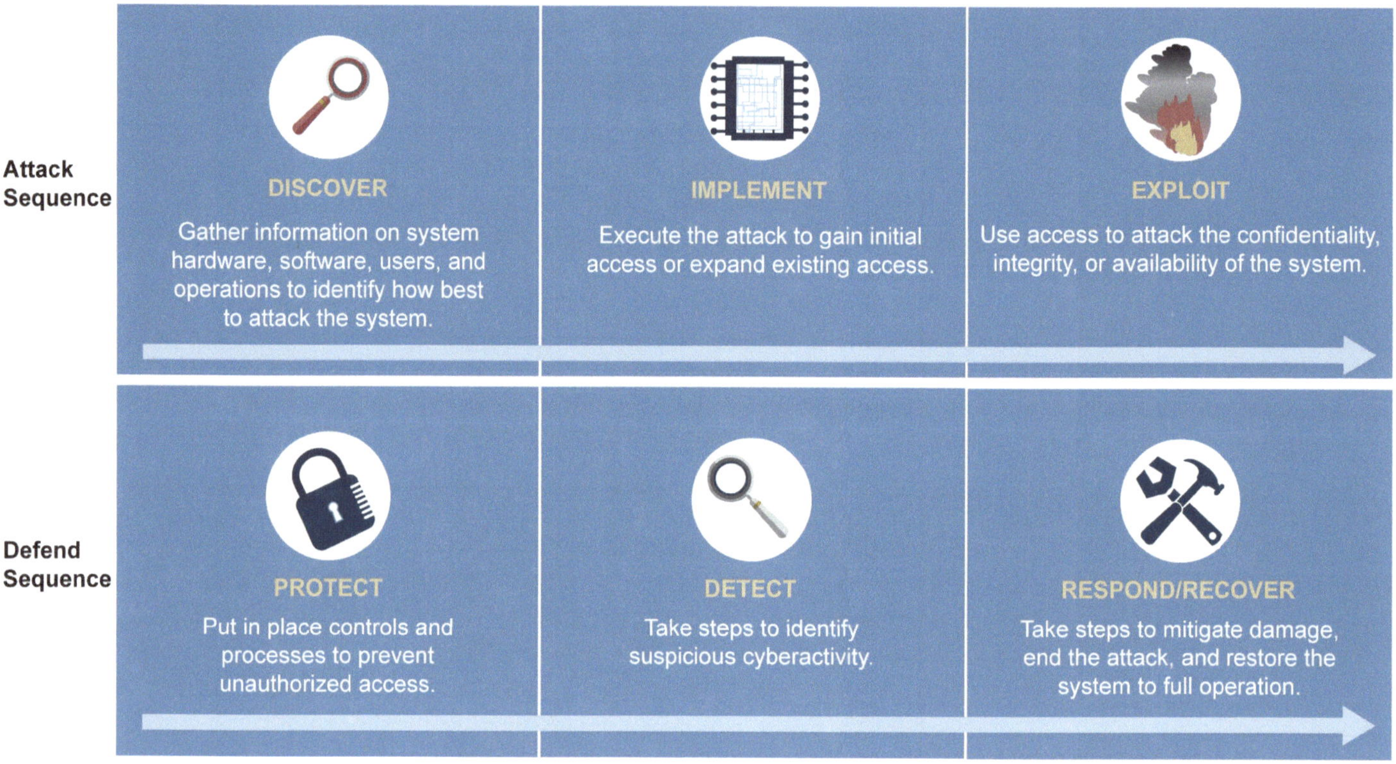

Attack Sequence		
DISCOVER	**IMPLEMENT**	**EXPLOIT**
Gather information on system hardware, software, users, and operations to identify how best to attack the system.	Execute the attack to gain initial access or expand existing access.	Use access to attack the confidentiality, integrity, or availability of the system.

Defend Sequence		
PROTECT	**DETECT**	**RESPOND/RECOVER**
Put in place controls and processes to prevent unauthorized access.	Take steps to identify suspicious cyberactivity.	Take steps to mitigate damage, end the attack, and restore the system to full operation.

Source: GAO analysis of Department of Defense information. | GAO-19-128

Attack Sequence: Discover → Implement → Exploit

A cyber attacker looks for ways to get around security controls in order to obtain full or partial control of the system. An attacker typically starts by learning as much as possible about the system—potentially through cyber reconnaissance—to identify vulnerabilities in the system. The more attackers know about the system, the more options they have when designing an attack. An attacker may identify a previously unknown vulnerability that the system owner is unaware of. Or the attacker could look for system components that had not applied known security updates—also called "patches." Developers of commercial components usually publicly announce any security patches and, ironically, provide a roadmap for an attacker to attack a system or component.[17]

An attack may not happen all at once—an attacker may find the easiest way to gain initial access and then look for ways to expand their access until they reach their ultimate goal. Even once they achieve full access to a system, an attacker may wait for an opportune time to attack the confidentiality, integrity, or availability of a system. Types of attacks are described in appendix II.

Example: Importance of Patching in a Timely Manner

In the 2017 **Equifax cyber attack**, personal data for over 145 million people were exposed. Attackers took advantage of a vulnerability in a commonly used web application to access Equifax's credit reporting system. A patch for the vulnerability was available in March, but Equifax had not applied it by the time of the attack—in mid-May.

Source: GAO-18-559 and Equifax statement. | GAO-19-128

Security Goals: Protect → Detect → Respond/Recover

The system owner wants to prevent, or at least limit, attempts to adversely affect the confidentiality, integrity, or availability of the system. The owner implements security controls such as firewalls, role-based access controls, and encryption to reduce the number of potential attack points. Many controls need to be designed into the system early in the development cycle. Ideally, the controls are designed to work together and there may be layers of controls that an attacker would have to defeat in order to gain control of the system—referred to as "defense in depth."

Protecting a system also includes administrative processes, such as requiring users to regularly change their passwords and applying patches on a regular schedule—referred to as cyber hygiene. However, no system can be completely secure, so system owners must also constantly monitor their systems for suspicious activity. Logging is a common system feature that automatically records system activity. Unusual patterns such as numerous failed log-in attempts from a remote location

Key Concepts

Role-based access entails allowing users to only access information and features necessary to carry out their job.

Encryption is a way of transforming information so that only authorized users are able to read it.

Source: GAO analysis of NSA information. | GAO-19-128

---

[17]For more information on patches, see the Department of Homeland Security's U.S. Computer Emergency Readiness Team's website, https://www.us-cert.gov/. See also GAO, *Information Security: Effective Patch Management is Critical to Mitigating Software Vulnerabilities,* GAO-03-1138T (Washington, D.C.: Sept. 10, 2003).

could indicate that an unauthorized person is trying to gain access to the system. Once such a cyber activity is detected, the system owner needs to take steps to end the attack and restore any system capabilities that were degraded as a result of the attacker's actions.

Attack Sophistication Levels

We reported in 2015 that federal and contractor systems face an evolving array of cyber-based threats, including criminals, hackers, adversarial nations, and terrorists.[18] Threats can range from relatively unskilled "script kiddies" who only use existing computer scripts or code to hack into computers, to well-resourced and highly skilled advanced threats who not only have sophisticated hacking skills, but also normally gather detailed knowledge of the systems they attack. Table 1 provides brief descriptions of the terminology DOD uses to categorize threats.

Table 1: Key Characteristics of Adversary Threat Tiers

Threat type	Description
Nascent	Little-to-no organized cyber capabilities, with no knowledge of a network's underlying systems or industry beyond publicly available open-source information.
Limited	Able to identify—and target for espionage or attack—easily accessible unencrypted networks running common operating systems using publicly available tools. Possesses some limited strategic planning.
Moderate	Able to use customized malware to conduct wide-ranging intelligence collection operations, gain access to more isolated networks, and in some cases creates limited effects against defense critical infrastructure networks.
Advanced	May conduct complex, long-term cyber attack operations that combine multiple intelligence sources to obtain access to high-value networks. May develop detailed technical and system knowledge of the target system to deploy more damaging cyber attacks.

Source: GAO analysis of Department of Defense (DOD) information. | GAO-19-128

DOD Weapon Systems Requirements and Acquisition Processes

Weapons systems are developed, acquired, and deployed within the defense acquisition system, a system of statutes and regulations. Subject to control of the DOD, the Army, Air Force, Navy, and Marine Corps by law have authority to "organize, train, and equip" their services.[19] Their decisions regarding what to develop and how best to do so are informed by documents and deliberations under DOD's requirements and acquisition processes respectively. Early in the acquisition lifecycle, the requirements process identifies what capabilities are needed and

---

[18]GAO, *Cybersecurity: Actions Needed to Address Challenges Facing Federal Systems*, GAO-15-573T (Washington, D.C.: Apr. 22, 2015).

[19]10 U.S.C. §§ 3013, 5013, 8013, 5042.

evaluates options to best meet those needs.[20] The acquisition process is a gated review process that assesses programs against established review criteria, such as the program's cost, schedule, performance, and whether the weapon system is ready to move forward in the acquisition process.[21] Numerous military-service entities are involved in these processes. Key enterprise-level organizations include the Joint Staff and Office of the Secretary of Defense organizations, such as the Office of the Under Secretary of Defense (Acquisition and Sustainment), Office of the Under Secretary of Defense (Research and Engineering), and the Director of Operational Test and Evaluation (DOT&E).

Organizations Responsible for Weapon Systems Cybersecurity

Just as many DOD organizations are responsible for weapon systems acquisitions, many have responsibilities related to cybersecurity during the acquisition process.[22] For example, program offices are responsible for planning and implementing cybersecurity measures for the system under development. Authorizing officials are responsible for overseeing programs' adherence to security controls and for authorizing a system's entry into operations based on the system having an acceptable level of cyber risk. At key decision points, the Office of the Under Secretary of Defense (Research and Engineering) is responsible for advising the Secretary of Defense and providing independent technical risk assessments that address a variety of topics, including the system's cybersecurity posture. Military test organizations conduct cybersecurity assessments of weapon systems. DOT&E oversees those tests and is funding research on the cybersecurity of some weapon system components that pose particular cybersecurity challenges.

Organizations that are traditionally associated with cybersecurity, such as NSA and Cyber Command, support some aspects of weapon systems cybersecurity. However, they are not responsible for reviewing the

Example: Increased Reliance on Software

In the 2015 **JEEP Cherokee cyber attack**, researchers remotely took physical control of a JEEP, including shutting off the engine and controlling the brakes. In 2016, we reported that electronic systems control multiple passenger vehicle functions and that vehicles include multiple interfaces that leave them vulnerable to cyber attacks.

Researchers studied a JEEP to understand its systems, including the characteristics of its software code and its "CAN Bus," which connects to units that control core vehicle functions. They remotely accessed an Internet-connected component and used it as an initial entry point to access the vehicle's CAN Bus, which then allowed them to control many of the JEEP's functions.

Source: GAO-16-350 and industry report. | GAO-19-128

---

[20]Department of Defense, *Manual for the Operation of the Joint Capabilities Integration and Development System* (Feb. 12, 2015).

[21]See, for example, DOD Instruction 5000.02, *Operation of the Defense Acquisition System* (Jan. 7, 2015)(incorp. change 3, eff. Aug. 10, 2017).

[22]For more information about organizations responsible for DOD weapon system acquisitions, see GAO, *Acquisition Reform: DOD Should Streamline Its Decision-Making Process for Weapon Systems to Reduce Inefficiencies,* GAO-15-192 (Washington, D.C.: Feb. 24, 2015); and *Weapon System Acquisitions: Opportunities Exist to Improve the Department of Defense's Portfolio Management,* GAO-15-466 (Washington, D.C.: Aug. 27, 2015).

designs of most weapon systems to identify potential vulnerabilities, although NSA officials said that they will provide advice to acquisition programs if asked to do so. More information about these roles and responsibilities is included in appendix III.

Multiple Factors Make Weapon Systems Cybersecurity Increasingly Difficult, but DOD Is Just Beginning to Grapple with the Challenge

Multiple factors contribute to the current state of DOD weapon systems cybersecurity, including: the increasingly computerized and networked nature of DOD weapons, DOD's past failure to prioritize weapon systems cybersecurity, and DOD's nascent understanding of how best to develop more cyber secure weapon systems. Specifically, DOD weapon systems are more software and IT dependent and more networked than ever before. This has transformed weapon capabilities and is a fundamental enabler of the United States' modern military capabilities. Yet this change has come at a cost. More weapon components can now be attacked using cyber capabilities. Furthermore, networks can be used as a pathway to attack other systems. We and others have warned of these risks for decades. Nevertheless, until recently, DOD did not prioritize cybersecurity in weapon systems acquisitions. In part because DOD historically focused on the cybersecurity of its networks but not weapon systems themselves, DOD is in the early stage of trying to understand how to apply cybersecurity to weapon systems. Several DOD officials explained that it will take some time, and possibly some missteps, for the department to learn what works and does not work with respect to weapon systems cybersecurity.

DOD Weapon Systems Are Increasingly Complex and Networked, Increasing Cyber Vulnerabilities

DOD's weapon systems are increasingly dependent on software and IT to achieve their intended performance. The amount of software in today's weapon systems is growing exponentially and is embedded in numerous technologically complex subsystems, which include hardware and a variety of IT components, as depicted in figure 2.

Figure 2: Embedded Software and Information Technology Systems Are Pervasive in Weapon Systems (Represented via Fictitious Weapon System for Classification Reasons)

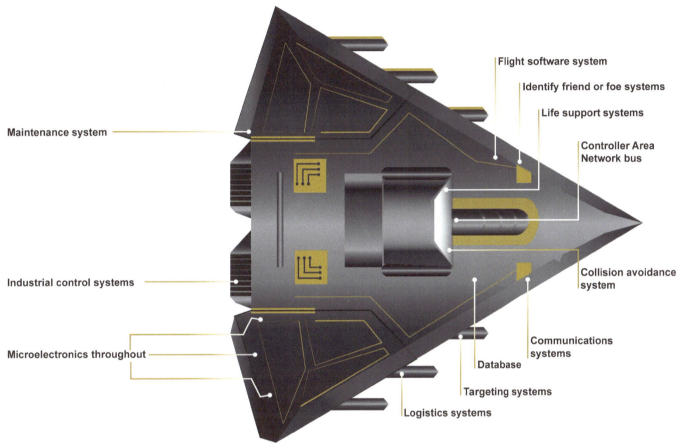

Source: GAO analysis of Department of Defense information. | GAO-19-128

Nearly all weapon system functions are enabled by computers—ranging from basic life support functions, such as maintaining stable oxygen levels in aircraft, to intercepting incoming missiles. DOD has actively sought ways to introduce this automation into weapon systems. For example, we have reported that for decades, the Navy has sought to reduce ship crew size based, in part, on the assumption that some manual tasks could be automated and fewer people would be needed to operate a ship.[23]

Yet this growing dependence on software and IT comes at a price. It significantly expands weapons' attack surfaces.[24] According to DOT&E, any exchange of information is a potential access point for an adversary. Even "air gapped" systems that do not directly connect to the Internet for security reasons could potentially be accessed by other means, such as USB devices and compact discs. Weapon systems have a wide variety of interfaces, some of which are not obvious, that could be used as pathways for adversaries to access the systems, as is shown in figure 3.

---

[23]GAO, *Navy Force Structure: Actions Needed to Ensure Proper Size and Composition of Ship Crews,* GAO-17-413 (Washington, D.C.: May 18, 2017); *Defense Acquisitions: Cost to Deliver Zumwalt-Class Destroyers Likely to Exceed Budget,* GAO-08-804 (Washington, D.C.: Jul. 31, 2008); *Defense Acquisitions: Improved Management Practices Could Help Minimize Cost Growth in Navy Shipbuilding Programs,* GAO-05-183, (Washington, D.C.: Feb. 28, 2005).

[24]GAO has also previously examined how reliance on software to control safety-critical and other functions leaves vehicles more vulnerable to cyber attacks. See GAO, *Vehicle Cybersecurity: DOT and Industry Have Efforts Under Way, but DOT Needs to Define Its Role in Responding to a Real-world Attack,* GAO-16-350 (Washington, D.C.: Mar. 24, 2016).

Figure 3: Weapons Include Numerous Interfaces That Can Be Used as Pathways to Access the System (Represented via Fictitious Weapon System for Classification Reasons)

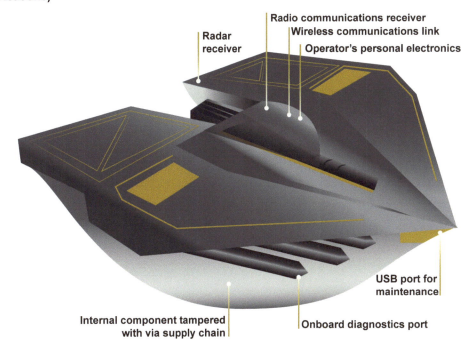

Radar receiver

Radio communications receiver

Wireless communications link

Operator's personal electronics

USB port for maintenance

Internal component tampered with via supply chain

Onboard diagnostics port

Source: GAO analysis of Department of Defense information. | GAO-19-128

Example: Importance of Network Segmentation

In the 2013 **Target cyber attack**, hackers obtained full names, contact information, credit card details, and other sensitive data for 41 million customers in part because of system design issues. Attackers initially accessed Target's network through a refrigeration, heating, and air conditioning subcontractor. Target's payment system was not directly connected to the Internet. However, reports indicate that because the payment system was on the same network as a nonpayment system, attackers were able to access it through that route.

Source: GAO analysis of Target statement and industry reports. | GAO-19-128

DOD systems are also more connected than ever before, which can introduce vulnerabilities and make systems more difficult to defend. According to the DSB, nearly every conceivable component in DOD is networked.[25] Weapon systems connect to DOD's extensive set of networks—called the DOD Information Network—and sometimes to external networks, such as those of defense contractors. Technology systems, logistics, personnel, and other business-related systems sometimes connect to the same networks as weapon systems. Furthermore, some weapon systems may not connect directly to a network, but connect to other systems, such as electrical systems, that may connect directly to the public Internet, as is depicted in figure 4.

---

[25]Department of Defense, Defense Science Board, *Task Force Report: Resilient Military Systems and the Advanced Cyber Threat,* (Washington, D.C.: Jan. 2013).

Figure 4: Weapon Systems Are Connected to Networks That May Connect to Many Other Systems (Notional Depiction for Classification Reasons)

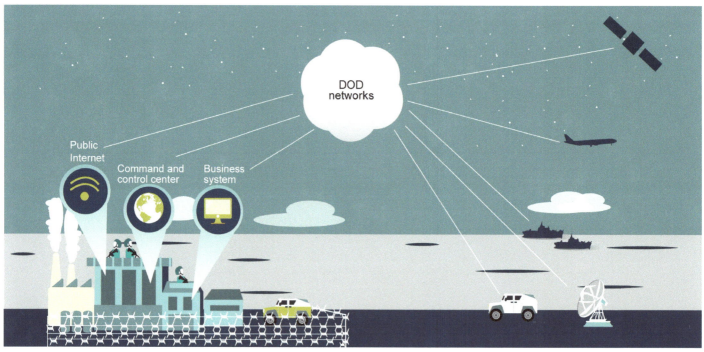

Source: GAO analysis of Department of Defense information. | GAO-19-128

These connections help facilitate information exchanges that benefit weapon systems and their operators in many ways—such as command and control of the weapons, communications, and battlespace awareness. If attackers can access one of those systems, they may be able to reach any of the others through the connecting networks. Many officials we met with stated that including weapon systems on the same networks with less protected systems puts those weapon systems at risk. Furthermore, the networks themselves are vulnerable. DOT&E found that some networks were not survivable in a cyber-contested environment and the DSB reported in 2013 that "the adversary is in our networks."[26]

---

[26]Survivable means that a system is able to maintain its critical capabilities under applicable threat environments. A cyber contested environment is when one or more adversaries attempt to change the outcome of a mission by denying, degrading, disrupting, or destroying our cyber capabilities, or by altering the usage, product, or our confidence in those capabilities. Defense Science Board, *Resilient Military Systems*.

Further complicating matters, weapon systems are dependent on external systems, such as positioning and navigation systems and command and control systems in order to carry out their missions—and their missions can be compromised by attacks on those other systems. A successful attack on one of the systems the weapon depends on can potentially limit the weapon's effectiveness, prevent it from achieving its mission, or even cause physical damage and loss of life.

Despite Warnings, Cybersecurity Has Not Been a Focus of Weapon Systems Acquisitions

We and other organizations have identified risks associated with increased reliance on software and networking since at least the early 1990s, as is shown in table 2.

Table 2: Examples of Warnings of Risks Associated with Increased Reliance on Software and Networking

Year	Details
1991	The National Research Council reported "as computer systems become more prevalent, sophisticated, embedded in physical processes, and interconnected, society becomes more vulnerable to poor system design, accidents that disable systems, and attacks on computer systems. Without more responsible design and use, system disruptions will increase, with harmful consequences for society."
1996	GAO reported that attackers had seized control of entire defense systems, many of which support critical functions, such as weapons systems, and that the potential for catastrophic damage was great. We explained that Internet connections make it possible for enemies armed with less equipment and weapons to gain a competitive edge at a small price.
1997	GAO reported that, though greater use of interconnected systems promises significant benefits in improved business and government operations, such systems are much more vulnerable to anonymous intruders, who may manipulate data to commit fraud, obtain sensitive information, or severely disrupt operations.
2004	GAO reported that while building a network based on Internet protocols is expected by the Department of Defense (DOD) to provide a more viable path to achieve interoperability and enable more dynamic and flexible information sharing, it also exposes DOD to the same vulnerabilities that all users of the Internet face, and increases the opportunity for potential attackers with limited knowledge and technical skills to cause a great deal of damage.
2007	The Defense Science Board (DSB) reported that DOD has become increasingly dependent for mission-critical functionality upon highly interconnected, globally sourced, information technology of dramatically varying quality, reliability and trustworthiness… this growing dependency is a source of weakness exacerbated by the mounting size, complexity, and interconnectedness of its software programs.
2013	DSB warned that in today's world of hyper-connectivity and automation, any device with electronic processing, storage, or software is a potential attack point and every system is a potential victim–including our own weapons systems.

Source: National Research Council, GAO, and DSB. | GAO-19-128

GAO-19-128 Weapon Systems Cybersecurity

Nevertheless, DOD has only recently begun prioritizing weapon systems cybersecurity. Instead, for many years, DOD focused cybersecurity efforts on protecting networks and traditional IT systems, such as accounting systems, rather than weapons. Experts we interviewed as well as officials from program offices, the Office of the Secretary of Defense, and some military test organizations explained that, until around 2014, there was a general lack of emphasis on cybersecurity throughout the weapon systems acquisition process. Others have reported similar findings. For example, the DSB reported in 2013 that although DOD had taken great care to secure the use and operation of the hardware of its weapon systems, it had not devoted the same level of resources and attention to IT systems that support and operate those weapons and critical IT capabilities embedded within the weapon systems.[27] The National Research Council reported in 2014 that much broader and more systematic attention to cybersecurity was needed in the acquisition process and that the Navy was in the "crawl" stage of a "crawl-walk-run" journey.[28] Similarly, the Navy reported in 2015 that there was a lack of attention to cybersecurity in the acquisition process and platform IT systems were not engineered with cybersecurity as a key component.[29]

In the past, consideration of cybersecurity was not a focus of the key processes governing the development of weapon systems. It was not a focus of key acquisition and requirements policies nor was it a focus of key documents that inform decision-making. For example, until a few years ago, DOD's main requirements policy did not call for programs to factor cyber survivability into their key performance parameters.[30] Key performance parameters are the most important system capabilities, called "requirements," that must be met when developing weapon systems. They are established early on in an acquisition program and drive system design decisions. They are also used as a benchmark to measure program performance and are reviewed during acquisition decisions and other oversight processes. Because cybersecurity key

---

[27]Defense Science Board, *Resilient Military Systems.*

[28]Unclassified statements from classified report. National Research Council of the National Academies, *Navy Cyber Defense Capabilities.*

[29]Unclassified statement from classified Navy report.

[30]See Department of Defense, *Manual for the Operation of the Joint Capabilities Integration and Development System,* (Jan 19., 2012) and 2015 update. Chapter 3 of this report discusses changes to this manual in 2015 to incorporate cybersecurity considerations.

performance parameters were not required, Joint Staff officials and some program officials said that many current weapon systems had no high-level cybersecurity requirements when they began, which in turn limited emphasis on cybersecurity during weapon system design, development, and oversight.[31] In addition, Joint Staff officials said that, historically, cybersecurity was not a factor in analyses of alternatives. This analysis is an important early step in acquiring a new weapon system and informs decisions about the relative effectiveness, costs, and risks of potential systems that could be developed.[32] By not considering cybersecurity in these analyses, decisions about which system to develop were made without consideration of whether one proposed system might be more inherently vulnerable from a cyber perspective than others.

Programs' lack of cybersecurity requirements may have also contributed to challenges with incorporating cybersecurity into weapon systems testing. Specifically, DOT&E and service test agencies said that prior to around 2014, program offices tried to avoid undergoing cybersecurity assessments because they did not have cybersecurity requirements and therefore thought they should not be evaluated. Furthermore, test officials said that many within DOD did not believe cybersecurity applied to weapon systems. As a result, fewer cybersecurity assessments were conducted at that time in comparison to recent years.

By not incorporating cybersecurity into key aspects of the requirements and acquisition processes, DOD missed an opportunity to give cybersecurity a more prominent role in key acquisition decisions. Numerous officials we met with said that this failure to address weapon systems cybersecurity sooner will have long-lasting effects on the department. Due to this lack of focus on weapon systems cybersecurity, DOD likely has an entire generation of systems that were designed and built without adequately considering cybersecurity. Bolting on cybersecurity late in the development cycle or after a system has been deployed is more difficult and costly than designing it in from the beginning. Not only is the security of those systems and their missions at risk, the older systems may put newer systems in jeopardy. Specifically, if DOD is able to make its newer systems more secure, but connects them to older systems, this puts the newer systems at risk. Furthermore, even if

---

[31]The Joint Staff has enterprise-level responsibilities related to the requirements process, including identifying, assessing, validating, and prioritizing capability needs.

[32]See the Defense Acquisition Guidebook.

they are not connected, if the newer systems depend on the older systems to help fulfill their missions, those missions may be at risk.

DOD Is Still Learning How to Address Weapon Systems Cybersecurity

DOD is still determining how best to address weapon systems cybersecurity given weapon systems' different and particularly challenging cybersecurity needs. Although there are similarities between weapon systems and traditional IT systems, DOD has acknowledged that it may not be appropriate to apply the same cybersecurity approach to weapon systems as traditional IT systems. RAND reported and several program officials we met with stated that DOD's security controls were developed with IT systems, and not weapon systems, in mind.[33] DOD policies and guidance acknowledge that tailoring may be warranted, but they do not yet specify how the approaches to the security controls should differ.

Key Concept

Industrial control system is a general term that encompasses several types of control systems including supervisory control and data acquisition systems, distributed control systems, and programmable logic controllers. Industrial control systems monitor or control other systems and processes and may be used to automate tasks such as opening and closing valves.

Source: GAO analysis of NIST information. | GAO-19-128

DOD is still in the process of determining how to make weapon system components with particular cyber vulnerabilities as secure as possible. For example, many weapon systems use industrial control systems to monitor and control equipment, and like computers, they include software. Many weapon systems use such systems to carry out essential functions. For example, a ship may use industrial control systems to control engines and fire suppression systems. According to NIST, industrial control systems were originally designed for use in trusted environments, so many did not incorporate security controls.[34] Government and industry reports state that attacks on these systems are increasing. However, DOD officials said that program offices may not know which industrial control systems are embedded in their weapons or what the security implications of using them are. Over the past few years, DOD has begun funding work to improve its understanding of how to best secure these systems. In addition, Office of the Secretary of Defense officials informed us that, in response to section 1650 of the National Defense Authorization Act for Fiscal Year 2017, they are working to better understand the dependency of industrial control systems on mission impact, including

---

[33]RAND, *Improving the Cybersecurity of U.S. Air Force Military Systems Throughout Their Life Cycles* (Santa Monica, Calif.: 2015).

[34]NIST 800-82, Revision 2. *Guide to ICS Security: Supervisory Control and Data Acquisition (SCADA) Systems, Distributed Control Systems (DCS), and Other Control System Configurations such as Programmable Logic Controllers (PLC)* (May 2015).

GAO-19-128 Weapon Systems Cybersecurity

other key infrastructure nodes that could be vulnerable to a cyber attack and have significant impact to mission accomplishment.[35]

Several weapon system-specific factors make it important to tailor cybersecurity approaches, but also make cybersecurity difficult. Because weapon systems can be very large, complex, systems of systems with many interdependencies, updating one component of a system can impact other components. A patch or software enhancement that causes problems in an email system is inconvenient, whereas one that affects an aircraft or missile system could be catastrophic. Officials from one program we met with said they are supposed to apply patches within 21 days of when they are released, but fully testing a patch can take months due to the complexity of the system. Even when patches have been tested, applying the patches may take additional time. Further, weapon systems are often dispersed or deployed throughout the world. Some deployed systems may only be patched or receive software enhancements when they return to specific locations. Although there are valid reasons for delaying or forgoing weapon systems patches, this means some weapon systems are operating, possibly for extended periods, with known vulnerabilities.

Key Concept

Vulnerability chaining is when attackers take advantage of multiple vulnerabilities—which could be low or moderate risk in isolation—to perform a more significant attack on a system.

Source: NIST. | GAO-19-128

Exacerbating matters, some program offices may also not yet have a solid understanding of the cybersecurity implications of their systems' designs, including their systems' connectivity. This situation makes it difficult to secure the system. Experts and officials from some test organizations we met with stated that programs have generally not understood the multitude of ways that information flows in and out of their systems, although this may be improving. Several program officials we met with felt that weapon systems were more secure than other types of systems and noted that they typically did not have direct connections to the Internet. In fact, weapon systems have more potential avenues of attack than may be apparent, such as radio communications receivers and radar receivers.[36] Furthermore, the National Research Council reported in 2014 that individual warfare domains do not fully grasp risks within their own domain, let alone those that can be introduced through

---

[35]National Defense Authorization Act for Fiscal Year 2017, Pub. L. No. 114-328, § 1650 (2016) called for DOD to submit to Congress a plan to evaluate the cyber vulnerabilities of DOD's critical infrastructure.

[36]See figure 3.

GAO-19-128 Weapon Systems Cybersecurity

other domains.[37] For example, if a space system is connected to a land system—even indirectly—an attacker may be able to move from one to the other or limit the operations of one by attacking the other.

Tests Revealed that Most Weapon Systems Under Development Have Major Vulnerabilities, and DOD Likely Does Not Know the Full Extent of the Problems

We found that from 2012 to 2017, DOD testers routinely found mission-critical cyber vulnerabilities in nearly all weapon systems that were under development. Using relatively simple tools and techniques, testers were able to take control of these systems and largely operate undetected. In some cases, system operators were unable to effectively respond to the hacks. Furthermore, DOD does not know the full scale of its weapon system vulnerabilities because, for a number of reasons, tests were limited in scope and sophistication.

Weapon Systems Cybersecurity Assessments Identified Mission-Critical Vulnerabilities

Nearly all major acquisition programs that were operationally tested between 2012 and 2017 had mission-critical cyber vulnerabilities that adversaries could compromise. DOT&E's 2017 annual report stated that tests consistently discovered mission-critical vulnerabilities in acquisition programs, echoing a similar finding by the DSB in 2013 about DOD IT systems and networks. Cybersecurity test reports that we reviewed showed that test teams were able to gain unauthorized access and take full or partial control of these weapon systems in a short amount of time using relatively simple tools and techniques.[38] We saw widespread examples of weaknesses in each of the four security objectives that cybersecurity tests normally examine: protect, detect, respond, and recover.

---

[37]Unclassified sentence from classified report. National Research Council of the National Academies, *Navy Cyber Defense Capabilities*. Warfare domains include: land, sea, air, space, and information.

[38]Operational assessments focus on systems that are in the later stages of development and help inform fielding decisions. Programs have the opportunity to resolve vulnerabilities prior to fielding.

Protect

Key Concepts

An **insider** is a user who is authorized to use a system (e.g., has a username and password) and has physical access to all or parts of a system.

A **near-sider** is an unauthorized user who has physical access to all or part of a system. For example, someone taking a tour of a Navy ship would be a near-sider.

A **remote user** is not authorized to use the system and does not have physical access to the system.

Source: DOD. | GAO-19-128

Example: Poor Password Management

The 2016 **cyber attack on Dyn,** a company that serves as a key intermediary in directing Internet traffic, disabled websites, such as Twitter, Netflix, and CNN and brought down the Internet in some regions. The attack used malware to search the Internet for unsecured devices, such as those that used factory-default usernames and passwords, and then used those devices to send junk traffic to online targets until they could not function.

Source: Congressional and industry reports. | GAO-19-128

Test Teams Easily Took Control

Test teams were able to defeat weapon systems cybersecurity controls meant to keep adversaries from gaining unauthorized access to the systems. In one case, it took a two-person test team just one hour to gain initial access to a weapon system and one day to gain full control of the system they were testing. Some programs fared better than others. For example, one assessment found that the weapon system satisfactorily prevented unauthorized access by remote users, but not insiders and near-siders. Once they gained initial access, test teams were often able to move throughout a system, escalating their privileges until they had taken full or partial control of a system. In one case, the test team took control of the operators' terminals. They could see, in real-time, what the operators were seeing on their screens and could manipulate the system. They were able to disrupt the system and observe how the operators responded. Another test team reported that they caused a pop-up message to appear on users' terminals instructing them to insert two quarters to continue operating. Multiple test teams reported that they were able to copy, change, or delete system data including one team that downloaded 100 gigabytes, approximately 142 compact discs, of data.

Test Teams Needed Only Basic Tools

The test reports indicated that test teams used nascent to moderate tools and techniques to disrupt or access and take control of weapon systems. For example, in some cases, simply scanning a system caused parts of the system to shut down. One test had to be stopped due to safety concerns after the test team scanned the system. This is a basic technique that most attackers would use and requires little knowledge or expertise. Poor password management was a common problem in the test reports we reviewed. One test report indicated that the test team was able to guess an administrator password in nine seconds.[39] Multiple weapon systems used commercial or open source software, but did not change the default password when the software was installed, which allowed test teams to look up the password on the Internet and gain

---

[39]One DOD test official we spoke to said that the time it took to break a password or access a system is not a useful metric for measuring cybersecurity. This official noted that a determined adversary could dedicate months or years to breaking into a system and with that time horizon, there is no meaningful distinction between breaking a password in a few hours or a few days. We have included this example, not as a measure of overall security, but to illustrate the ease with which the test team was able to access the system.

administrator privileges for that software. Multiple test teams reported using free, publicly available information or software downloaded from the Internet to avoid or defeat weapon system security controls.

Security Controls Were Insufficient

Test reports we reviewed make it clear that simply having cybersecurity controls does not mean a system is secure. How the controls are implemented can significantly affect cybersecurity. For example, one test report we reviewed indicated that the system had implemented role-based access control, but internal system communications were unencrypted. Because the system's internal communications were unencrypted, a regular user could read an administrator's username and password and use those credentials to gain greater access to the system and the ability to affect the confidentiality, integrity, or availability of the system.

Programs Had Not Addressed Some Previously Identified Vulnerabilities

Program offices were aware of some of the weapon system vulnerabilities that test teams exploited because they had been identified in previous cybersecurity assessments. For example, one test report indicated that only 1 of 20 cyber vulnerabilities identified in a previous assessment had been corrected. The test team exploited the same vulnerabilities to gain control of the system. When asked why vulnerabilities had not been addressed, program officials said they had identified a solution, but for some reason it had not been implemented. They attributed it to contractor error. Another test report indicated that the test team exploited 10 vulnerabilities that had been identified in previous assessments.

Detect

Test reports we reviewed indicated that test team activities were not detected at all during some assessments, including one case in which the test team operated for several weeks without being detected. One test report indicated that test team activities were not discovered even though the test team was deliberately "noisy" and was not trying to hide its activities. In other cases, intrusion detection systems correctly identified test team activities as suspicious, but users were unaware of the detection.[40] One test team emulated a denial of service attack by rebooting the system, ensuring the system could not carry out its mission for a short period of time.[41] Operators reported that they did not suspect a cyber attack because unexplained crashes were normal for the system. Another test report indicated that the intrusion detection system correctly identified test team activity, but did not improve users' awareness of test team activities because it was always "red." Warnings were so common that operators were desensitized to them.

A common way to detect cyber activity is to review logs of system activity looking for unusual occurrences.[42] Multiple test reports indicated that test team activity was documented in system logs, but operators did not review them. One test report noted that the system had no documented procedures for reviewing logs.

Respond/Recover

Multiple test reports indicated that operators did not effectively respond to test team activities. In multiple tests, operators did not respond because, as noted above, they were simply unaware of the test team activities. In some cases, however, operators were unable to effectively respond even when they identified or were notified that the test team had carried out an attack.[43] One test report indicated that operators identified test team intrusion attempts and took steps to block the test team from accessing the system. However, the test team was able to easily circumvent the steps the operators took. In another case, the test team was able to compromise a weapon system and the operators needed outside assistance to restore the system.

---

[40]Intrusion detection systems are software intended to identify, and possibly mitigate, unusual system activity. For example, they may look for attempts to change system settings or unusual file transfers in or out of the system. The intrusion detection system may automatically respond or notify users of suspicious activity.

[41]A denial of service attack prevents or impairs authorized use of networks, systems, or applications by exhausting resources.

[42]Operating systems and applications often track system activity and store it in a log file. For example, a system may log failed attempts to access the system. System administrators can then search the logs for suspicious activity. For example, repeated failed log-in attempts could indicate that someone is probing the system and attempting to guess a user's password.

[43]Test teams attempt to evaluate operators'/systems' ability to protect, detect, respond, and recover from a cyber attack. When test team activities were not detected, the test team notified operators in order to assess their response.

DOD Has Limited Insight into Weapon Systems Cybersecurity

DOD does not know the full extent of its weapon systems cyber vulnerabilities due to limitations on tests that have been conducted. Cybersecurity assessments do not identify all vulnerabilities of the systems that are tested. This is, in part, because cybersecurity assessments do not reflect the full range of threats that weapon systems may face in operation. Test teams reported that they portray realistic threats and environments. However, the nature of tests imposes limitations on testers that do not apply to potential adversaries. For example, DOD officials said that most cybersecurity assessments are conducted over a few days to a few weeks. One test report indicated that the cybersecurity assessment was cut short due to external factors so the test team only had 41 hours to work with the system. In contrast, DOD officials we spoke to said that a determined adversary could spend months or years targeting our systems.

Further, because test teams have a limited amount of time with a system, they look for the easiest or most effective way to gain access, according to DOD officials we met with and test reports we reviewed. They do not identify all of the vulnerabilities that an adversary could exploit. DOT&E noted that longer-term tests generally identify more cyber vulnerabilities than shorter tests. DOD officials we spoke to said that the department has increased the amount of long-term assessments it conducts in recent years. Weapon systems cybersecurity assessments may also be limited in the types of attacks that are portrayed so entire categories of vulnerabilities are not currently addressed in some cyber assessments. The test reports we reviewed tended to portray nascent to moderate threats and generally did not target special components like industrial control systems and non-Internet enabled devices which our adversaries could target. Similarly, counterfeit parts pose cybersecurity risks to weapon systems, but were not within the scope of the cybersecurity tests that we reviewed.[44]

System-specific limitations can also affect test results. Officials from one service test agency noted that in at least one case, they could not fully assess a system's cybersecurity because portions of the system's

---

[44]GAO has previously examined DOD's use of counterfeit parts. See GAO, *Counterfeit Parts: DOD Needs To Improve Reporting and Oversight To Reduce Supply Chain Risk,* GAO-16-236 (Washington, D.C.: Feb. 16, 2016); and *Defense Supplier Base: DOD Should Leverage Ongoing Initiatives in Developing Its Program To Mitigate Risk of Counterfeit Parts,* GAO-10-389 (Washington, D.C.: Mar. 29, 2010).

GAO-19-128 Weapon Systems Cybersecurity

networks and data were proprietary. The system utilized the contractor's corporate networks, which the test team was not allowed to attack. In several tests, a weapon system's connections to external systems were either limited or had to be simulated. One test report we reviewed noted that the test team was not allowed to use classified networks to attack a weapon system due to security concerns. Another test was conducted in a lab environment so the test team had to simulate external communications. Although there are practical reasons for limiting the duration and scope of cybersecurity assessments, these limitations mean that DOD may not fully understand the extent of weapon system cyber vulnerabilities, as is reflected in figure 5.

Figure 5: Vulnerabilities that the Department of Defense Is Aware of Likely Represent a Small Amount of Actual Vulnerabilities Due to Limitations in Cybersecurity Testing

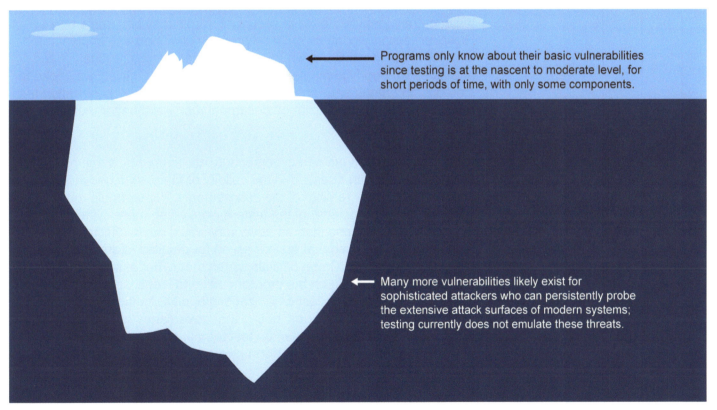

Programs only know about their basic vulnerabilities since testing is at the nascent to moderate level, for short periods of time, with only some components.

Many more vulnerabilities likely exist for sophisticated attackers who can persistently probe the extensive attack surfaces of modern systems; testing currently does not emulate these threats.

Source: GAO analysis of Department of Defense information. | GAO-19-128

Program Offices May Have False Sense of Confidence in the Security of Their Programs

Many program officials we met with indicated that their systems were secure, including some with programs that had not had a cybersecurity assessment. Some systems have not yet undergone testing either because they are not far enough along in the acquisition process, because they were fielded prior to DOD's emphasis on penetration testing, or out of concern that cybersecurity tests would interfere with operations. Systems that have not been tested are not necessarily more or less secure than systems that have been assessed. DOD does not know the extent to which these systems have cyber vulnerabilities.

Program officials cited the security controls they applied as the basis for their belief that their systems were secure. For example, officials from a DOD agency we met with expressed confidence in the cybersecurity of their systems, but could not point to test results to support their beliefs. Instead, they identified a list of security controls they had implemented. However, security controls must be properly designed and implemented in order to be effective. As we noted earlier, test teams routinely found and defeated poorly implemented security controls. Officials we spoke to stated that controls are necessary, but not sufficient, and penetration test results—rather than compliance documentation—are better indicators of a system's security.

For programs that have had cybersecurity assessments, some program officials we met with questioned the validity of the results because of concerns about the realism of the assessments. For example, officials from one program noted that the testers were given more system information and access than an adversary would have. Officials from another program noted that testers asked for detailed information about the system's design. These officials stated that cyber assessments were unrealistic if they relied on the program office to identify problem areas for the test team. However, test organizations and NSA officials we met with dismissed these observations, noting that adversaries are not subject to the types of limitations imposed on test teams, such as time constraints and limited funding—and this information and access are granted to testers to more closely simulate moderate to advanced threats.

DOD Has Begun Taking Steps to Improve Weapon Systems Cybersecurity

Over the past few years, DOD has taken several major steps to improve weapon systems cybersecurity. DOD issued and updated numerous policies and guidance to improve the department's development of cyber resilient systems. These include improvements such as specifying that cybersecurity policies apply to weapon systems and requiring more focus on cybersecurity throughout a weapon system's acquisition life cycle. DOD and Congress have also begun promising initiatives to help DOD improve its understanding of its weapon systems cyber vulnerabilities and take steps to mitigate their risks. However, DOD faces barriers that may limit its ability to achieve desired improvements. For example, DOD is struggling to hire and retain cybersecurity personnel, who are essential to implementing these changes. In addition, DOD faces barriers to information sharing, which hinder its ability to share vulnerability and threat information within and across programs. To improve the state of weapon systems cybersecurity, it is essential that DOD sustain its momentum in developing and implementing key initiatives.

DOD Has Issued and Updated Policies and Guidance

Since 2014, DOD has issued or updated at least 15 department-wide policies, guidance documents, and memorandums intended to promote more cyber secure weapon systems, some of which are highlighted in table 3.[45]

---

[45]In addition, the military services have also issued policies and guidance related to weapon systems cybersecurity, but we are not addressing them in this report.

Table 3: Timeline of Key Department of Defense (DOD) Policy and Guidance Changes to Improve Weapon Systems Cybersecurity

Year	Key changes[a]
2014	• DOD replaces its "Information Assurance" instruction with **Department of Defense Instruction (DODI) 8500.01, Cybersecurity**. Identifies responsibilities and procedures for managing cybersecurity risk throughout the system lifecycle. Risk should be managed commensurate with the importance of supported missions and the value of potentially affected information or assets. Emphasizes operational resilience, including information and service availability. • DOD replaces its Information Assurance Certification and Accreditation Process instruction with **DODI 8510.01, DOD Risk Management Framework (RMF) for Information Technology (IT)**, which also calls for a risk-based approach to cybersecurity. Requires—and aligns with DOD's acquisition process—a six-step process, including: categorizing the system, selecting security controls, implementing controls, assessing controls, authorizing the system, and monitoring the controls. • DOD issues a memorandum, **Procedures for Operational Test and Evaluation of Cybersecurity in Acquisition Programs**, requiring that operational testing for major weapon systems reflect cyber threats with the same rigor as other threats.
2015	• DOD issues **The Department of Defense Cyber Strategy**, which states DOD's intent to: (1) assess and initiate improvements to the cybersecurity of current and future weapons systems, (2) mandate cybersecurity standards for future weapons systems, and (3) update acquisition and procurement policies and practices to promote effective cybersecurity throughout a system's life cycle. • DOD modifies its main requirements policy—the **Joint Capabilities Integration and Development System Manual**. The mandatory system survivability key performance parameter, which is intended to ensure the system maintains its critical capabilities under applicable threat environments, is revised so that it requires systems to operate in a degraded cyber environment. • DOD issues the **DOD Cybersecurity Test and Evaluation Guidebook**, which provides cybersecurity test and evaluation information to support RMF and cybersecurity across the acquisition life cycle. • DOD issues the **DOD Program Manager's Guidebook for Integrating the Cybersecurity Risk Management Framework into the System Acquisition Lifecycle**. Among other things, the guidebook includes sections that walk through examples of how the RMF could be applied to a weapon system and how cybersecurity should be incorporated into the acquisition process.
2017	• DOD updates its key instruction governing the acquisition process, **DODI 5000.02, Operation of the Defense Acquisition System**. Its new cybersecurity enclosure states that cybersecurity is a requirement for all programs and must be fully considered and implemented in all aspects of acquisition programs across the life cycle. The instruction provides details of how this should be done, focusing on the roles of the program manager. • DOD issues the **Cyber Survivability Endorsement Implementation Guide** to help sponsors articulate cyber survivability requirements. Officials are to assign their program a risk category based on the system's mission, cyber dependence, capabilities of threats, and impact of system compromise to the mission. Programs are to tailor controls to their category. The category should inform capability decisions in key documents such as the analysis of alternatives and requirements documents.

Source: GAO analysis of DOD information. | GAO-19-128

[a]Some of these documents have subsequently been updated. Due to our focus on showing major DOD policy and guidance changes related to cybersecurity, we do not include those updates here.

One of the more significant changes is that DOD's existing cybersecurity policies now explicitly apply to weapon systems. DOD officials said the department has had cybersecurity policies in place for decades, but applied them to weapon systems only in the past few years. For example, DOD's Risk Management Framework (RMF) is similar to its predecessor—DOD's Information Assurance Certification and

Accreditation Process—which called for application of an extensive series of controls to protect DOD networks and information systems. However, RMF applies these controls more widely to weapon systems cybersecurity. Another important change is that, in recognition that systems cannot be 100 percent secure, DOD has begun to emphasize cyber resiliency in some of its policies. The idea behind cyber resiliency is to identify and protect key elements of a system to ensure that they can continue to operate, possibly with limited capabilities, during a cyber attack.[46] This entails designing in features such as durability, redundancy, and added protections for certain components.

Lastly, key policies that govern the requirements and acquisition processes now address cybersecurity. These changes have the potential to bring greater attention to cybersecurity in weapon systems acquisitions. Rather than being treated as distinct from the acquisition process, cybersecurity is to be integrated into key acquisition activities, such as requirements development, technology maturation, and testing. Examples of this, as called for in various policies, include the following:

- **Requirements.** Identify cybersecurity requirements and how the information flows into, out of, and through the systems. This helps identify the system's attack surface and informs the system's design and cybersecurity controls. Cybersecurity should become part of the requirements trade space.[47]

- **Technology maturation.** Focus early prototyping in part on buying down cybersecurity risks prior to system development. Cybersecurity controls should be applied and assessed during prototyping to evaluate cyber risks and inform down-selection and adjustment of requirements.[48]

---

[46]Without resiliency, a cyber attack could immediately kill a mission and have other effects. For example, in some IT situations, it may be possible to shut down a system and reboot or troubleshoot issues. However, in the case of an aircraft, for example, these options are problematic.

[47]Department of Defense, *Manual for the Operation of the Joint Capabilities Integration and Development System,* 2015; and *Cyber Survivability Endorsement Implementation Guide* (2017).[48]Department of Defense, *DOD Program Manager's Guidebook for Cybersecurity* (Sept. 2015).

[48]Department of Defense, *DOD Program Manager's Guidebook for Cybersecurity* (Sept. 2015).

- **Developmental testing.** Test the cybersecurity of weapon systems as they are developed, including integration of larger subsystems and, ultimately, the entire system. Perform cybersecurity assessments in representative operating environments during developmental testing.

- **Operational testing.** Conduct operational cybersecurity testing of weapon systems to include other systems that exchange information with the system under test (system-of-systems to include the network environment), end users, administrators, and cyber defenders. Reflect representative cyber threats.[49]

These extensive changes to policies and guidance, which adopt a similar risk-based framework to that already generally in place government-wide, appear to be a step in the right direction to increase the department's emphasis on weapon systems cybersecurity. However, they are also relatively new for DOD, so it is too early to assess whether they are resulting in improved weapon systems cybersecurity. For example, changes to the requirements process apply primarily to new programs so it could be many years before systems that have gone through the new process undergo operational testing and are fielded.

DOD Has Undertaken Initiatives, in Part Directed by Congress, to Help Understand and Address Weapon Systems' Cyber Vulnerabilities

Section 1647 of the National Defense Authorization Act for Fiscal Year 2016 requires the Secretary of Defense to evaluate the cyber vulnerabilities of each DOD weapon system by the end of 2019 and develop strategies to mitigate risks stemming from those vulnerabilities.[50] In response to this direction and The DOD Cyber Strategy, which also calls for DOD to assess and initiate improvements to the cybersecurity of current and future weapons systems, DOD is taking steps to improve its understanding of its weapon systems' vulnerabilities, determine how to mitigate risks from those vulnerabilities, and inform future development of more secure systems. The Office of the Under Secretary of Defense (Acquisition and Sustainment) is leading this initiative in collaboration with military test organizations. DOD is compiling existing vulnerability information and conducting some new tests to provide information about the cybersecurity posture of individual systems, concentrating mostly on fielded systems. These assessments are important, in part because some of those systems did not undergo cybersecurity testing prior to fielding

---

[49]Office of the Secretary of Defense, *Procedures of Operational Test and Evaluation of Cybersecurity in Acquisition Programs* (Aug. 1, 2014). Updated April 3, 2018.

[50]National Defense Authorization Act for Fiscal Year 2016, Pub. L. No. 114-92, § 1647 (2015).

and DOD does not have a permanent process in place to periodically assess the cybersecurity of fielded systems. Furthermore, vulnerabilities and risks can change after fielding as system software becomes obsolete.

As part of this initiative, for two mission areas, the Office of the Under Secretary of Defense (Acquisition and Sustainment) has been trying to incorporate cybersecurity into large scale military exercises to take a more integrated look at impacts of vulnerabilities across systems. The goal is to understand how vulnerabilities in some systems may affect DOD's ability to achieve its mission and to identify what other options are available to complete a mission if certain capabilities were disabled or degraded. This work is also important, but for different reasons. DOD's developmental and operational tests focus primarily on vulnerabilities in individual systems rather than across broader mission areas. However, as previously discussed, attackers do not necessarily limit themselves to one system and may move from one system to others. Furthermore, DOD has not previously had a process in place to examine how cyber attacks on one system could affect entire missions.

Taken together, the system-specific and mission-focused activities could help DOD develop a more comprehensive understanding of its cybersecurity posture—the overall strength of its cybersecurity. Officials working on these assessments plan to use what they learn to help inform the acquisition of future weapon systems. Specifically, they plan to share lessons with DOD test organizations, the Office of the Chief Information Officer, Office of the Under Secretary of Defense (Research and Engineering), and others in the Office of the Under Secretary of Defense (Acquisition and Sustainment).

Similarly, the military services have established weapon system cybersecurity-focused offices to improve their cybersecurity posture, which are described briefly in table 4.

Table 4: Military Service Initiatives Focusing on Weapon Systems Cybersecurity

Service	Organization and year established	Mission
Navy	CYBERSAFE, 2015	Aims to help assure survivability and resiliency of critical warfighting information technology and system components and processes. Provides enhanced assurance requirements for systems and components.
Air Force	Cyber Resiliency Office for Weapon Systems, 2017	Focuses on mission-level cyber risk analysis, integrating cyber into systems engineering, developing a cyber-savvy workforce, and increasing the integration of cyber intelligence. Aims to ingrain cyber resiliency into Air Force culture in order to maintain mission effective capability under adverse conditions.
Army	Task Force Cyber Strong, 2017	Conducted a deep-dive, Army-wide review to assess the service's cyber needs, strengths, weaknesses, and assets. With this information, they plan to develop a holistic approach to address weapon systems and industrial control systems cybersecurity.

Source: GAO analysis of Department of Defense Information. | GAO-19-128

Although all of these activities promise to help DOD improve its cybersecurity posture over time, they are also relatively new for DOD. They will need sustained momentum to achieve changes over the lifecycle of acquisition programs, so it is too early to tell if they will be successful over the long term. According to multiple agency officials and our analysis of policy and guidance changes since 2014, DOD leadership has become more aware of cybersecurity issues over the past several years and has driven many of these cybersecurity activities. However, our prior work has found sustained leadership support of DOD initiatives to be key to maintaining their momentum.[51] We also reported that there is risk that DOD will not fully implement some tasks it has begun to improve weapon systems cybersecurity if leadership does not continue to monitor their progress.[52] For example, we reported in 2017 that DOD's Principal Cyber Advisor closed out the task on assessing weapon systems called for under The DOD Cyber Strategy. We recommended that the Cyber

[51]GAO, *Department of Defense: Sustained Leadership Is Critical to Effective Financial and Business Transformation*, GAO-06-1000T (Washington, D.C.: Aug. 3, 2006); and *Department of Defense: Further Actions Are Needed to Effectively Address Business Management Problems and Overcome Key Business Transformation Challenges*, GAO-05-140T (Washington, D.C.: Nov. 18, 2004).

[52]GAO, *Defense Cybersecurity: DOD's Monitoring of Progress in Implementing Cyber Strategies Can Be Strengthened*, GAO-17-512 (Washington, D.C., Aug. 1 2017).

Advisor modify criteria for closing tasks to reflect whether tasks have been implemented and re-evaluate tasks that have been previously determined to be completed.

DOD Faces Systemic Barriers to Improving Weapon Systems Cybersecurity

DOD faces barriers that will challenge its ability to develop more cyber resilient weapon systems and make it more difficult for DOD's recent policy changes and new initiatives to be as effective as possible.

Cybersecurity Workforce Challenges

DOD struggles to hire and retain cybersecurity personnel, particularly those with weapon systems cybersecurity expertise. Our prior work has shown that maintaining a cybersecurity workforce is a challenge government-wide and that this issue has been a high-priority across the government for years.[53] Program officials from a majority of the programs and test organizations we met with said they have difficulty hiring and retaining people with the right expertise, due to issues such as a shortage of qualified personnel and private sector competition. Test officials said that once their staff members have gained experience in DOD, they tend to leave for the private sector, where they can command much higher salaries. According to a 2014 RAND study, personnel at the high end of the capability scale, who are able to detect the presence of advanced threats, or finding the hidden vulnerabilities in software and systems, can be compensated above $200,000 to $250,000 a year, which greatly exceeds DOD's pay scale.[54]

Even when cybersecurity positions are filled, it may not necessarily be with the right expertise. Officials from some program offices said that general cybersecurity expertise is not the same as weapon systems cybersecurity expertise. For example, officials said that professional IT certifications are not the same as systems security engineering expertise,

[53]GAO, *Cybersecurity Human Capital: Initiatives Need Better Planning and Coordination,* GAO-12-8 (Washington, D.C.: Nov. 29, 2011); *Federal Workforce: OPM and Agencies Need to Strengthen Efforts to Identify and Close Mission-Critical Skills Gaps* GAO-15-223 (Washington, D.C.: Jan. 30, 2015); *Cybersecurity: Actions Needed to Strengthen U.S. Capabilities,* GAO-17-440T (Washington, D.C.: Feb. 14, 2017); and *Cybersecurity: Federal Efforts are Under Way that may Address Workforce Challenges,* GAO-17-533T (Washington, D.C.: April 4, 2017).

[54]RAND Corporation, *Hackers Wanted: An Examination of the Cybersecurity Labor Market,* (2014). We did not examine the various federal workforce flexibilities that could help resolve these recruiting and retention issues.

which is essential to designing cyber-resilient systems. According to various program officials, weapon systems cybersecurity is a specialized area. Cybersecurity subject matter experts require knowledge of (1) DOD's acquisition process; (2) technical knowledge of the specific weapon system—such as radar or aircraft, and (3) cybersecurity knowledge. However, it is difficult to hire and maintain a workforce with the needed knowledge due to its highly specialized nature. Without this expertise, it will be difficult for programs to effectively implement cybersecurity policies and guidance. For example, the RMF allows programs to determine which controls are most appropriate to apply, but a knowledgeable workforce is necessary for making such decisions.

DOD has various efforts underway to recruit and develop the skills of DOD's cybersecurity workforce, according to several DOD officials. For example, the services are aiming to recruit cybersecurity analysts by using internships and engaging in partnerships with secondary schools and universities. In addition, the services are developing and offering courses to grow expertise within their existing acquisition workforce. DOD is determining how to share specialized expertise related to weapon systems cybersecurity. Specific efforts related to this include the Cyber Developmental Test Cross Service Working Group that meets quarterly and invites industry expertise to present cutting edge techniques as well as a "capture the flag" competition, which will now be offered to other services as well. In addition, Navy Systems Commands employees participate in periodic regional cyber competitions to hone knowledge learned in classroom environments and use training funds to pursue additional or higher degrees and cyber certificate programs.

Barriers to Information Sharing

Officials from many of the offices we interviewed, as well as the National Research Council, DSB, and RAND have expressed concerns about barriers to information sharing. It is difficult to find the correct balance between protecting information, so that it is not accessible to potential adversaries, and sharing it, so that DOD has an informed workforce. For example, classification is important because it protects information about vulnerabilities, and in some cases, intelligence methods. Access to information about vulnerabilities makes it easier for potential adversaries to attack DOD systems. Similarly, limiting the distribution of classified information to those who have the need to know is likewise important because it reduces the likelihood that internal and external threats will access it. Although DOD officials explained that there is no DOD-wide cybersecurity classification guidance, Air Force guidance and DOD officials indicated that vulnerabilities in fielded systems are typically classified as at least Top Secret or Top Secret/Sensitive Compartmented Information, and details of threats are more restricted.[55] This high level of classification for weapon systems cyber vulnerabilities and threats helps protect sensitive information, but it makes it difficult for DOD to share information about aspects of weapon systems cybersecurity with cybersecurity personnel across DOD. For example, some experts told us that flawed designs can still be found in new systems if their designers were not aware that they resulted in vulnerabilities in other systems. More generally, because they are not sharing vulnerability and threat information across programs, programs are unaware of their full risk exposure and DOD may have less insight into vulnerabilities across its weapon systems portfolio. Officials from most organizations we spoke to, including NSA, acknowledged challenges with sharing information across all levels within DOD. Examples of these challenges are listed in table 5.

Table 5: Challenges with Sharing Information about Cyber Vulnerabilities and Threats

Challenge	Example
Limited insight into connected systems	Officials from a program with a heavily connected weapon system stated that their system is only as secure as its weakest link, but they do not have information on the vulnerabilities of systems it connects to due to classification.
Problems obtaining details about attacks	If a weapon system experienced a cyber attack, DOD program officials would not be provided specific details of that attack from the intelligence community due to the type of classification of that information.
Cannot leverage information across programs	Office of the Secretary of Defense officials who are responsible for assessing weapon system cyber vulnerabilities and developing strategies to mitigate their risks are not allowed to share what they learn about specific vulnerabilities with other programs.
Uninformed operators	Some system operators, including defenders, do not have the clearances to access threat or vulnerability information.
Inability to obtain classified information while deployed	Some Navy ships do not have the facilities to receive or store highly classified information.

Source: Department of Defense officials. | GAO-19-128

Although limitations to information sharing can lead to inefficiencies and other challenges, DOD has so far opted to favor protection of

---

[55]DOD uses classification to protect national security information. "TOP SECRET" is a classification level above SECRET and is applied to information, the unauthorized disclosure of which reasonably could be expected to cause exceptionally grave damage to the national security; Sensitive Compartmented Information is a special category of classification for information about or from intelligence sources, methods, or analytical processes.

information—perhaps because the stakes are so high if it does not. As we mentioned previously, one of the reasons potential adversaries collect information on weapon systems is because the better they understand a weapon system, and especially what vulnerabilities it may have, the more options they have to attack it. Reports over the years about cyber espionage attacks on defense contractors show that concerns about protecting sensitive information are warranted.[56]

Agency Comments

We provided a draft of this report to DOD for review and comment. DOD provided technical comments, which we incorporated where appropriate.

We are sending copies of this report to the appropriate congressional committees; the Secretary of Defense; and the Secretaries of the Army, Navy, and Air Force. In addition, the report will be available at no charge on GAO's website at http://www.gao.gov.

If you or your staff have any questions about this report, please contact me at 202-512-4841 or chaplainc@gao.gov. Contact points for our Offices of Congressional Relations and Public Affairs may be found on the last page of this report. GAO staff who made major contributions to this report are listed in appendix IV.

Cristina T. Chaplain
Director, Contracting and National Security Acquisitions

---

[56]See, for example, GAO, *Computer Security: Hackers Penetrate DOD Computer Systems,* GAO/T-IMTEC-92-5 (Washington, D.C.: Nov. 20, 1991); and Larry M. Wortzel, *Cyber Espionage and the Theft of U.S. Intellectual Property and Technology,* Testimony before the House of Representatives Committee on Energy and Commerce Subcommittee on Oversight and Investigations, 113th Cong., 1st sess., July 9, 2013.

GAO-19-128 Weapon Systems Cybersecurity

Appendix I: Scope and Methodology

To identify factors that contribute to the current state of Department of Defense (DOD) weapon systems cybersecurity, we reviewed reports published from 1991 to the present on software, information technology, networking, and weapon systems from the National Research Council, the Defense Science Board, GAO, DOD's Director of Operational Test and Evaluation, DOD's Joint Chiefs of Staff, and the RAND Corporation. To inform our discussion of networking, we also reviewed concepts of operations for selected systems of systems. To determine the extent to which DOD focused on cybersecurity in weapon system acquisitions, we analyzed selected information assurance, acquisition, requirements, and testing policies and guidance. For this and all other objectives, we conducted interviews with or obtained written responses from the following organizations:

- Office of the Secretary of Defense organizations: Office of the Director, Operational Test and Evaluation; Office of the Deputy Assistant Secretary of Defense for Developmental Test and Evaluation; Office of the Chief Information Officer including the Defense Information Systems Agency; Office of the Chairman of the Joint Chiefs of Staff; Office of the Under Secretary of Defense (Acquisition and Sustainment); and Office of the Under Secretary of Defense (Research and Engineering).

- Military service test organizations: Air Force Operational Test and Evaluation Center, Army Operational Test and Evaluation Command, Navy's Commander Operational Test and Evaluation Force, and Marine Corps Operational Test and Evaluation Activity.

- Selected program offices reflecting a purposeful sample of nine major defense acquisition program offices. We identified a variety of program offices to represent each service, multiple domains, and programs that are extensively connected to other weapons systems. We are not listing the names of these offices for sensitivity reasons.

- Other key DOD organizations with cybersecurity responsibilities: the National Security Agency, Defense Information Systems Agency, and U.S. Cyber Command.

- Selected organizations with cybersecurity expertise, referred to as "experts" in the report: Carnegie Melon's Software Engineering Institute, the MITRE Corporation, the RAND Corporation, Pacific Northwest National Laboratory, Sandia National Laboratory, and Renaissance Strategic Advisors. We selected these based on their research or roles advising DOD on weapon systems cybersecurity-related topics.

To identify vulnerabilities in weapon systems under development, we reviewed cyber assessment reports of selected weapon systems conducted between 2012 and 2017. We selected at least one program from each service as well as different types of weapon systems (e.g., aircraft vs ships vs communication systems). To gain further insights into assessment findings and understand their limitations, we interviewed officials from the Office of the Secretary of Defense and military test service organizations. We discussed the cybersecurity of individual programs, implementation of controls, and assessment findings with program offices. We also interviewed officials from several organizations with cybersecurity expertise to discuss weapon system vulnerabilities and test limitations. Vulnerabilities for specific weapon systems are classified, so we have not identified the programs covered in these test reports. The examples we cite are unique to each weapon system and are not applicable to all weapon systems. Furthermore, cybersecurity assessment findings are as of a specific date so vulnerabilities identified during system development may no longer exist when the system is fielded.

To determine the steps DOD is taking to develop more cyber resilient weapon systems, we analyzed key DOD information assurance/cybersecurity, acquisition, requirements, and testing policies and guidance that have been updated since 2014 to better address weapon systems cybersecurity. We selected 2014 because DOD began revising several policies at that time. These include DOD's Risk Management Framework, Department of Defense Instruction 8500.01, Cybersecurity; the Department of Defense Instruction 5000.2, Operation of the Defense Acquisition System; DOD Program Manager's Guidebook for Integrating the Cybersecurity Risk Management Framework into the System Acquisition Lifecycle; the Joint Capabilities Integration and Development System Manual; the Cyber Survivability Endorsement Implementation Guide; and the DOD Cybersecurity Test and Evaluation Guidebook. To identify barriers DOD faces in developing cyber resilient systems and implementing updated cybersecurity policies and guidance, we interviewed Office of the Secretary of Defense, military service test organizations, selected program offices, other DOD organizations, experts, and operators.

We took additional precautions to avoid revealing sensitive information. We illustrated some concepts using notional depictions. In some cases, we were deliberately vague and excluded details from examples to avoid identifying specific weapon systems. We also presented examples of publicly known attacks in sidebars to illustrate how poor cybersecurity can enable cyber attacks. DOD conducted a security review of the report and approved it for public release.

Appendix II: Examples of Types of Cyber Attacks

Table 6: Examples of Types of Cyber Attacks

Type of attack	Description
Denial of service	An attack that prevents or impairs the authorized use of networks, systems, or applications by flooding the system with data and exhausting resources
Distributed denial of service	A variant of the denial of service attack that uses numerous hosts to perform the attack.
Malware	Also known as malicious software, malware refers to a program that is inserted into a system, usually covertly, with the intent of compromising the confidentiality, integrity, or availability of the victim's data, applications, or operating system or otherwise annoying or disrupting the victim. Examples of malware include logic bombs, Trojan horses, ransomware, viruses, and worms.
Man-in-the middle	A form of active eavesdropping attack in which the attacker intercepts to read or modify data communications to masquerade as one or more of the entities involved.
Pass-the-hash	The attacker captures an encrypted version of a username and password in order to authenticate to a server or service. The attacker does not have to decrypt the username and password (i.e., they do not actually know what they are), yet can still use them to log in to a system.
Social engineering	An attempt to trick someone into revealing confidential information (e.g., a password) that can be used to attack systems or networks. Examples include: phishing—when the attacker masquerades as a legitimate business or reputable person via an e-mail or website to obtain certain information; spear-phishing—when phishing attacks are closely tailored to the audience; and whaling—phishing that targets high ranking members of organizations.
Spoofing	False signal is broadcasted with the intent to mislead the victim receiver, such as a Global Positioning System or email user.
Structured query language injection	An attack that involves the alteration of a database query, usually in a web-based application, which can be used to read, edit, or delete information in a database.
Supply chain	An adversary inserts vulnerabilities in hardware or software in order to manipulate those systems at the developer, assembly, or designer's location. Can be activated at a later point in time without direct access by the attacker.
War driving	The method of driving through cities and neighborhoods with a wireless-equipped computer—sometimes with a powerful antenna—searching for wireless networks potentially to exploit.
Zero day exploit	An exploit that takes advantage of a security vulnerability previously unknown to the general public. In many cases, the exploit code is written by the same person who discovered the vulnerability. By writing an exploit for the previously unknown vulnerability, the attacker creates a potent threat since the compressed timeframe between public discoveries of both makes it difficult to defend against.

Source: GAO analysis of data from the National Institute of Standards and Technology, the National Security Agency, United States Computer Emergency Readiness Team, and industry reports. | GAO-19-128

Appendix III: Roles and Responsibilities for Cybersecurity in the Department of Defense

Cybersecurity Roles and Responsibilities

The Department of Defense (DOD) is responsible for defending the U.S. homeland and interests from attack, including those that occur in cyberspace and has developed capabilities for cyber operations. In order to achieve this objective, the department must be able to defend its own networks, systems, and information from cyber attack. To establish a cybersecurity program to protect and defend DOD information and information technology, DOD has assigned some of its components and senior officials with a variety of cybersecurity responsibilities, some of which are described below.

Table 7: Selected Roles and Responsibilities for Cybersecurity in the Department of Defense

DOD Senior Officials and Components	Key Cybersecurity Roles and Responsibilities
Authorizing official	Senior official or executive with the authority to formally assume responsibility for operating an information system at an acceptable level of risk to organizational operations (including mission, functions, image, or reputation), organizational assets, individuals, other organizations, and the nation.
Defense Information Systems Agency	Provides, operates, and assures command and control, information sharing capabilities, and a globally accessible enterprise information infrastructure for DOD and other partners.
Deputy Assistant Secretary of Defense, Developmental Test and Evaluation	Focused on improving developmental test and evaluation planning and execution, building the professional workforce, and providing data-driven support to the DOD Components to improve acquisition outcomes.
Director, Operational Test and Evaluation	Issues policy and procedures, oversees operational test planning, and independently evaluates and reports on test results.
DOD Chief Information Officer	Principal staff assistant and senior advisor to the Secretary of Defense for information technology, information resources management, and efficiencies. Oversees management of DOD cyberspace information technology and cybersecurity workforce. Responsible for policy, oversight, and guidance for the architecture and programs related to DOD's networking and cyber defense.
DOD component heads	Responsible for ensuring DOD systems under their authority comply with the Risk Management Framework.
Milestone decision authority	Designated individual with overall responsibility for a program. Has authority to approve entry of an acquisition program into the next phase of the acquisition process and is to be accountable for cost, schedule, and performance reporting to higher authorities.
National Security Agency	Provides support to DOD components for assessing threats to, and vulnerabilities of, information technologies, and provides cybersecurity products and services to support of DOD components.
Under Secretary of Defense for Acquisitions, Technology, and Logistics[a]	Oversees all DOD cyber-capability acquisitions. Oversees DOD cybersecurity research and engineering investments, including research at the National Security Agency. Ensures information assurance training of the DOD acquisition workforce.
U.S. Cyber Command	Provides mission assurance for the operation and defense of the DOD information environment, defends the nation against strategic threats to U.S. interests and infrastructure, and supports the achievement of joint force commander objectives.

Source: DOD policies and guidance. | GAO-19-128

[a]In response to Section 901 of the National Defense Authorization Act for Fiscal Year 2017 (Pub. L. No. 114-328), DOD is restructuring the office of the Under Secretary of Defense, Acquisition, Technology and Logistics. Effective February 1, 2018, that office was reorganized into two separate offices: the Under Secretary of Defense (Research and Engineering) now advises the Secretary on key investments to retain technical superiority based on the analytical rigor and understanding of risk associated with these technologies; and the Under Secretary of Defense (Acquisition and Sustainment) advises the Secretary on all matters regarding acquisition and sustainment and is involved in the oversight of individual programs as required. We describe the Under Secretary of Defense for Acquisition, Technology and Logistics' role here because cybersecurity roles of the new offices have not yet been fully documented in policy.

Appendix IV: GAO Contact and Staff Acknowledgments

GAO Contact	Cristina T. Chaplain (202) 512-4841 or chaplainc@gao.gov.
Staff Acknowledgements	In addition to the contact named above, Raj Chitikila (Assistant Director), Brandon Booth, Laura Greifner, L.T. Holliday, Katherine Pfeiffer, James Tallon, Jacqueline Wade, and Robin Wilson made key contributions to this report. Assistance was also provided by Tommy Baril, Nabajyoti Barkakati, Mark Canter, Virginia Chanley, Kurt Gurka, Joseph Kirschbaum, Jeff Knott, Duc Ngo, and Gregory Wilshusen.

www.ingramcontent.com/pod-product-compliance
Lightning Source LLC
Chambersburg PA
CBHW041432050326
40690CB00002B/514